Don't Skip the Introduction- You Need It

Your passion is the one default thought about who you desire to become or whom you have always wish you were. That deep desire that burns inside of you. Your passion is also that one thing everybody else notices about you. You know that conversation that goes something like this; if I were you I would do this because you are so good at it. That moment in the conversation that sparks in your heart. One thing you should know is your passion is already there. It is a natural ability or gift if you will that defines you. Looking at the greatest talents in this world from Steve Jobs to Oprah Winfrey to NBA coach Pat Riley there passion for their gifts manifested within them stirring them up, challenging them to not play on the low ground but to take their passion to new heights. Nothing from beyond the grave could stop them from becoming the greatest. I am not a fan of boxing but one thing I loved about Mohammed Ali was his ability to motivate himself to dig deep within and say to himself and the world that he was the greatest. He changed his philosophy along with everyone else's philosophy about his ability to indeed become one of the most well-known boxers in the world. Your passion to succeed or fail is based upon your ability to BELIEVE! And defining that belief to encompass every aspect of your core being. If the mind, heart and soul don't line up with your philosophy or your beliefs then that crack in the lineup will defeat your ability to aim for the stars. Which leads me to the next point. In the film "A Knight's Tale" a young man was transformed by the words of his father "you can change your stars." Understanding that where you start has no bearing on the journey to becoming a star. We have heard countless stories of rags to riches and rich to richer; with that said we have seen many dreams never make it on the board. The idea, the vision and the plan didn't line up with their belief about their core being. They played on the negative which outnumbered their ability to break the chains that kept them from achieving. Those dreams are on someone else's production line. Something I have learned about myself is that my thoughts about myself, my past and my low income background was so strong that I would talk myself out of promotions, dreams and success. Literally, I would have these conversations that would eventually destroy any motivation I had to take the next steps to success. Instead, I would develop a core plan for failure. My thoughts, my past and my low income background lined up with failure and I did it well. So I had to ask myself if all those things lined to help me successfully fail, then why those thoughts couldn't be transformed to line up with my success. Have you ever failed and congratulated yourself because it was a well thought out plan? Every day we don't live out our dreams that is exactly what we do. Pat yourself on the back because the first step to success is admitting your failures. Because once you understand how you failed then that plan can be reversed to execute a plan for achievements, success and high earnings. Obviously, you have feel that this is your season and that's why you have purchased this book. Congratulation. It's time to discover and define your passion.

Facing the Truth

The truth shall set you free! It's true. When we desire to tap into our dreams the first thing every business organization states as the first thing to do is write down your business plan. I am going to be the first one to stomp out that tired old statement. As we know hundreds of businesses fail within the first year; there is a reason. Most people believe because a business owner didn't write their business plan carefully or possibly financial down trends in their industry others believe it's the inability to market effectively. All of those may be contributing factor but the truth is failure began long before you sat down to write down your business plan. If you were to pull that dusty old thing and review your plan you will discover all of your beliefs about yourself. You wrote down all of your weaknesses, failures and downfalls. From the beginning your plan was based upon all of those factors. I remember sitting in front of the counselor at the small business development program and listening to them speak about how to develop a business plan. The broke down the components every brick- a- brack and bone of how to start your business. They never really had a plan to assist you in going any further. It was just something for you to brainstorm. I started counting how many times I had been to these types of meeting and finding myself back in the start position over and over again.

Something has to be wrong. There is a factor that isn't fitting into the equation. Researching every successful person I could think of there was nothing that separated us. Yet, there was something that was different. A key factor that I and thousands of others were missing. What made Bill Gates, Steve Jobs, Oprah Winfrey and Victoria Secret are the best in the business and their respective industries. Were they smarter, did they have more money, friends or the hidden "it" factor. Struggling for years to determine what set them apart. So I developed a bucket list for business attempting and failing, attempting and failing. Defeated, I resolved they had the "it" chromosome, that genome that just made them better at achieving. For years, I had fixed my belief that this is all there is to life. I had been passed over for the "it" in my genes. It's over. So I through in the towel and became bitter, withdrawn and depressed. Life was not worth the effort. The daily disappointments of my life grew bigger and bigger crushing me under the throngs of life's spitter spatter. I had run out of gas and wasn't going to move beyond the mark.

Parenthood and Passion

Cause and effect are scientific facts except when you can break the genome code of failure. As I stated earlier there is more to developing your passion, your dream than a business plan. That is the "it" that is breaking or making you. Ding! Ding! a light came on in my brain. I remember it clearly. I had to return to work after my husband was diagnosed with heart failure. At this point my life was meaningless. There was only one thing I had learned over my life and that was how to raise successful, powerful and driven children. But that wasn't always the case. I had to re-develop a plan to become a successful parent. That meant, I had to change everything I believed, knew and grew up understanding. Once upon a time, I couldn't have been a worse parent. In fact, it was written down as the classic cause and effect cycle of life and I lived it out to the core. Don't get me wrong it wasn't my intention but that was the dysfunctional plan I understood. The children were great but I wasn't. I entered every possible bad relationship there was; becoming the poster child for what not to do in every form. It's the same for every drug dealer, alcoholic abusive and criminal behavior text book play that comes forth. The "it" was what the understood. How many times have you seen a drug dealer making dough and you wonder why they couldn't put those entrepreneurial skills into a legitimate business. The liar! Liar! that was written for them was so strong they walked onto the stage acting out every role defined for their character. It was built for them at a young age. This is what I changed in my parenting. I decided that if I wanted to become a successful parent I had to erase the diagram on the board of my brain. No matter what it had to go it wasn't working. Obviously, that plan preys upon the script that wasn't written. So I had to burn that to meaning the thoughts that were running through my mind. You ain't nothing. This played in every area of my life. As a minister, I was devalued on the pulpit because of my gender, background and strengths. I remember becoming ordained and never being invited to preach by the ordaining minister. Churches would look over me knowing I was ordained, knowing I could preach it and bring it. Yet, they would pass me over. I was so distraught over it that I sunk deeper into depression. I was angry. So, I just stopped. Then there was always the finger pointing. Someone always wanted to bring up your past but I never understood that when they bring up your past show them your future. But we will get back to that later. Facing your truth is about knowing who you are at the core of your being. Understanding what has kept you from success and helped you gravitate towards failure is the first step to developing your passion. You must get to the point where you define your failures. It's the soundtrack of your life. Who's blaming who for your own failures. Most of the time we have an excuse a person, place or situation that has torn away those dreams like a rapist in the dark who stalks his victim so does your thoughts. Many people never recover instead they become catatonic meaning they are unable to move forward or backward. You just stuck. How many times have you felt that in your life. Just stuck!

Weak at the Ankles...

The title of this paragraph says a lot. Your weakness makes you unable to stand up at all. One day, my family and I was in charge of a Christmas production at our church. We rehearsed two to three times a week. We wanted it to be fabulous. Several individuals were involved. We were excited. Then one night during rehearsal as we were going over the dance routine I fell to the ground an excruciating pain in my ankles hit me. I had never had any problems with my ankles before. I did every turn correctly. But at the end of rehearsal I couldn't stand up. I had to be wheeled out to the car. My husband and a precious friend put me in the car. When I got home my husband who had never seen me give in to anything couldn't believe I couldn't just hop my way to the door; he had to pick me up. For the first time in our lives together he realized I was in real pain. To this day I don't know why. But a few days later I recovered and was able to do the play. Years later, as I began to develop my passion I reflected back to this incident. Becoming weak at the ankles and what it can do to your entire body. If we don't define our weaknesses and failure we will never be able to cross over to the promise land. It is impossible to walk without your ankles which is the foundation of your ability to walk. When we think of walking with think of our feet but without our ankles we cannot move. Just like a business plan is the feet of our business the ankles are facing the truth of why we fail. We cannot move one step without it. I have watched hundreds get on their feet only to fall down in excruciating pain. The foundation to building your passion begins with the ankles of your business plan. Your *__Failures, Defeats and Weaknesses__*. Every plan has these key factors that must be addressed in order to overcome and develop a plan to eliminate those areas that have kept us from crossing over. This applies to every aspect of your life whether you are trying to lose weight, build a business or become the best employee in your field. Whatever your goals these three factors must be dealt with and dealt with truthfully. No one knows what is in the heart of man except God and that man. You know your weaknesses and what causes your defeats and failures better than anyone. In your precious time alone, reflect on those things that have kept you separated from your dreams. Write those things down, meditate upon them and discover why those thing have kept you from your dream. Most people would say write them down and forget about them but remember these three things play a factor in the development of your character and your ability to achieve or fail. Take each of those weaknesses and define how they have played into your defeats and failures. Understanding how your weaknesses defeat you and cause you to fail will help you to develop and execute a plan to meet the challenge when they arise. Get familiar with your weakness and revisit those defeats. Every great team that has ever won a state championship, every director or producer who has ever won an Emmy and every great actor who has ever won an award will tell you they had some weaknesses, failures and defeats they had to revisit in order to review where they went wrong. Once they understood that they were able to construct a play that would ultimately change their game from failure to success. This is vital to your success in the future. Again, this doesn't just apply to those wanting to start a business this is for anything that requires success or achievement on any level. If you want it you must introduce yourself to your weakness. One day, I was talking to a young woman which I often do so I asked her what is your Passion? She shrugged her shoulders which most of them do. So, I re-phrased the question as with many. If you could be anyone or do anything in this world without any hindrances what would that be? Suddenly, they begin spilling their guts. My response would go something like this. So why aren't you doing that. Immediately, they have more excuses than one could possibly dictate in one court hearing. Then I follow up with so why aren't you living your passion again? They will have this look on their face and respond with didn't you just hear what I said? Of course, but I just want to know why you aren't the person you really want to become? Removing their excuses reveals their weaknesses. My response is, allow me to answer that really quickly. Now that we know about all of the weaknesses that have caused you to fail what are you going to do about it? Chilling isn't it. Once you have blurped out all of the weaknesses in your plan you realized that most of them can be **fixed, transformed or managed.** Developing a plan to do any one of those things is possible. It just matter of knowing what they are. When an architecture develops his drawing they don't always see the problems until the plan actually goes into effect; once they begin to develop it the weaknesses that may cause the plan to fail or the obstacles that may cause it to be defeated in the offices can be overcome. The architecture will begin to work on stabilizing the plan to stave off any defects that may cause the building to collapse; in other words the weaknesses are defined in order to prevent defeat and failure. In order for you to develop a business plan for your life of success there must be a meeting with the three other factors that intermingle with *your Failures, Weaknesses and Defeats.* These three factors lies within your mind, heart and soul. The thoughts in your mind that remind you of what you can't do is your weakness. Your heart that accepts the failure and your soul which become distraught with the symphony of defeat are all working together to create the cycle that has plagued your life. ***If you want to live your passion define your weakness.***

Let's Review

- The first step in developing a business is confronting your issues.
- Discover what is causing your Failures, Weaknesses and Defeats
- Why have those issues defeated you
- Write down those things that have stolen your dreams
- Define the holes in your weaknesses
- Introduce yourself to those weaknesses, meditate upon them
- How do those three factors intermingle with your mind, heart and soul

The Unexpected Source

For every plan there is an obstacles. Like our weaknesses those darn obstacles can hinder our success if we don't have a plan to overcome those obstacles from the beginning. There is none that hasn't encountered obstacles in their lives. The difference is in how we deal with those obstacles that determines whether or not we can move forward. Being in business in some form or another over the past ten years has taught me a thing or two about obstacles. The first thing I learned is they will always be there. For every one obstacle that you overcome there will be another that raises it head. Being prepared on every perimeter on the course is the ultimate goal prior to wrapping up your business. In short, what are you going to do if your financial source runs out? What are you going to do if x doesn't match y? How will you remove the mountain standing in midst of your production. When going into business or developing a plan for our achievement we never think about those obstacles we only see the plan and jump right into it never expecting obstacles be lurking in the shadows. Believe they are there waiting for their moment on the stage of your plan. Once you know to plan for obstacles x will always match y because you have a plan for when x doesn't fit in the strand of your genome. Instead you will know how to change the course without so much as a stitch out of place. Just in case you don't understand what an obstacle is and how it differs from those three factors we discussed earlier let's define it right now. Unlike Failures, Weaknesses and Defeat obstacles only come once the plan is in effect. The moment you start on your journey. Those hairy cracks along the way that may cause you to stumble. In some cases, divert your plan into another direction. It's like writing a script for a particular actor who decides to back out of the role and now none of the words written for them fits any other actor in your repertoire. But, then that person comes along and says I can do it let me have it. That the x becoming an "A" sometimes what you planned isn't that best but in the end because of the obstacles that hindered the production a better plan arises to accomplish the goal making it a hit. In the movies, many times the first actor isn't always the best but the second choice can win the Emmy. The unexpected source may be the winner. When my husband and I began to launch our business there were a lot of unexpected factors that allowed us to navigate through some of the webs that hinders from achieving. Earlier in our marriage we were very inexperienced wide-eyed with dreams of glamour and glitz anything was possible. We would develop these elaborate ideas that would honestly take several thousands of dollars in six figure incomes to launch. We leaped into it hook line and sink! However, unlike the Titanic we would surface once more. We applied for grants, business loans, loans, signature loans everything we could imagine in order to launch our dreams.

When those things were revealed as false claims we were crushed. Later on, we began to develop other businesses and decided to re-vamp our business plan and go for the goal and request a loan. We never looked at the factors defined previously nor were we prepared for any obstacles. We had faith that the doors would be opened and we would like the dream. Once again, crushed. Several years later, we launched our ministry like we would any business again finding that it cost money to do those things. We had talent and we were out looking for other talents to express our talents. What we were looking for in our obstacles was someone to help us write our music, someone else to help type up our story, someone else to film it. We were looking for the distributors in our industries. We both had different gifts and interest investing in each other. Year after year we found ourselves in the same spot in the desert. Yep! That's the same mountain. So we broke off a piece of the mountain and sat on it for years looking right at the promise land but no way to get there because the mountain was still there. That same mountain in the heat of the desert an obstacle to our dreams. Until... Yes there is a until... we realized that our gifts and talents that we were searching for high and low we had been sitting on for years in the desert. We were the ones allowing the mountain to become an obstacle and just like we had broken a piece off the mountain to sit on we could keep breaking a piece off the mountain in order for it to be moved. Finally, we discovered a plan to the obstacles that had separated us from the road to success. So, we began to break bits and pieces off the mountain. We tackled every piece of it meeting it with determination. We broke off the piece to music by learning to play instruments and teaching our children so they could help us with that piece of the mountain. Then we released our first CD. Did it go platinum. NO! of course not but we broke that piece off and learned how to produce a CD. We bought the software we trained ourselves and became producers of our own music. Instead of looking for a publishing company we developed our own and I began to use my typing talents as a secretary to publish my own book not just one but several. That piece was taken from the mountain. We began to preach but we had no platform in which they would allow us to utilize the pulpit so we created our own radio station.

We continued to do this until the mountain was a pebble in the desert of our dreams. Suddenly the mountain was no longer an obstacles we had carved a pathway using the mountain as our stepping stones leading us to success. That's the difference between weaknesses, failures and defeat. An obstacle can be broken down into pieces eventually removing it's presence from your life. Every obstacle has a role on the road to your success. They are the orchestra or instrument that can be used to pave the way to your dreams. Remember there is no obstacle that cannot be broken down nor is there any obstacle that cannot help you get to your promise land. No matter what that mountain may be in your life you have the ability to chip away at it until it is removed. Never allow an obstacle to present itself as a weakness. It's not a thought it's an obstacle a force that is placed in your path. Everything placed in the path can be removed. Many times obstacles may mimic the three factors making it appear larger than it really is before your eyes. When an obstacles appears in your path it is your job to discern whether or not this fall into the category of the three factors or is this a mirage presenting itself as a major factor. Many dreams are derailed because we fail to discern if whether or not it an obstacle, weakness or a factor in our failures and defeats. Once you have learned to determine where that obstacle falls you can pick up your chainsaw and chop it into pieces. But don't be deceived into thinking those obstacles will be easy to break down. Some are large but once again, how and if it can be broken is based upon your determination to succeed. Don't let that obstacle become an excuse or the shrug in your shoulders as you shuffle around in the dirt. For many years, I spent too much time not being able to discern an obstacle from a defeat. I didn't understand that my obstacles became the excuse in which I could exit the plan to success. When an obstacle is allowed to fester and grow it can manifest into a great fear in your soul that will hinder you from picking up the ax and going for it. As we all know fear is paralyzing. It is part of that catatonic state I spoke of earlier that stops you sticking you in the ground. If you allow it your dreams can be hinder as we you watch it go down sinking into the darkness of quicksand. As I have learned over the years you cannot allow the obstacle to become fear in your life. I remember when we first tried launching our soap business the obstacle was my competition, finances and product. Although, I knew those things could be fixed, transformed and managed I decided to allow it to trick me into self-loathing. The obstacle had not only became a fear but it became a matter of self-confidence within myself. They had a better product, they were more informed on the industry and they had the financial backing to get it done. This paralyzed me into giving up my dreams. I didn't understand what role an obstacle played in my self-confidence nor did I understand how it could change the game. This is what is meant by everything about your dream can be fixed, transformed and managed. Instead of being paralyzed there was an opportunity for me to **fix** my product, **transform** my image and **manage** my finances. Your obstacle is an opportunity to become better at what you do and out perform your competition. Every business owner is always training the successor or in some cases their replacement. You have decide if you want to be the one by not allowing the obstacles to stop you in your track. You can do that by not walking up to the mountain and knocking it down which is how we become overwhelmed. Instead, break down the foundation bringing the mountain down to your size, then knock it down. In my case, it had to be knocked down quite a lot. I am very short but that mountain came tumbling down. Obstacles are meant to be removed that's it purpose to present itself, challenge you and allow you the opportunity to knock it down.

Let's Review

- What is an obstacle?
- Define the difference between an obstacle and a weakness, failure and defeat
- What is the purpose of an obstacle
- How can you remove an obstacle
- What are three thing you can do to remove the obstacle
- Obstacles can be transformed into this
  Developing Your Passion

The Origin of Dreams...

When dreams come true they have originated from a philosophy of in which a person has based their values, principles and belief systems upon. It is the core of their being. The dictionary has two defining definition in which I wholeheartedly believe is the essential proof of human nature and the answer to nature vs nurture. Let's take a look

1. Philosophy is defined as the critical study of basic principles and concepts of a particular branch of knowledge, especially with a view of improving or reconstituting them (Dictionary.com, Unabridged)

2. A system of principles for guidance in particular affairs (Dictionary.com, Unabridged)

   Every plan or dream incorporates an individual's philosophy. Your business cannot survive without some type of belief system. This will encompass everything you do in the present as well as in the future. This is because most of our dreams are launch from something we believe in an essential study of basic principles in which have developed, learned and incorporated into who we are as a person. Because of this we have dedicated our lives to improving and reconstituting thus redefining those principles whether positively or negatively. In turns these system of principles become the driving force in all of our personal, interpersonal and business affairs. These core belief is not solidified in your plan to achievement will cause a crack in your plan. These philosophy must be written down, re-defined and investigated to ensure they match up with your overall belief system. If you decide that this is not important you will quickly discover that what you are attempting to build has no basis. Whenever an election year comes about every political leader that decides to become a candidate regardless of the branch or political party spends years developing these core beliefs. The candidate that mostly aligns with American overall views based upon the percentages of those views will most likely win. There wins are based upon a philosophy whether to make a change or keep on the same track and those views are put through the fire by American of all backgrounds. The leaders selected undoubtly have been chosen because their branch of knowledge, study of basic principles, and concepts to improve and reconstitute our beliefs along with a system in which those principles will guide the affairs of all Americans becomes the winner. At any time, if those views change the candidate must change, adapt and re-define their views to match those of society. That same principles goes into your plan of achievement. It is important you spend some time developing your philosophy for your business model. This principle will guide you in choosing your team, selecting department leaders and those who will become your inner core. Those whom surround you in your endeavor must encompass these core values. When we don't surround ourselves with like-minded individuals we find ourselves in a situation where someone is working against you in every manner. They will question your abilities essentially they have a different belief system and methodology in which they would rather encompass. These individual's will usually reveal themselves early in the process. However, sometimes those individuals can be clever holding on to get inside before dismantling your dreams from within. Believe it or not, I learned this philosophy in the church. There is always someone seeking to undermine what you are attempting to build. I am not knocking the church but when you are in any situation where a group must gather together whether at work, church, home and yes even in your own family then you will encounter this problem. There is always someone wanting and waiting to take it all from you in an instant. They have waited for this very moment. That is why it is important to not just look at those individuals background as the only factor but more importantly what are their beliefs. Yes, there will always be some differences that can be utilize to solidify your dreams but don't just focus on who they were before but rather who are they now and what do you see in them that closely mirrors your system of beliefs. Most companies spend a lot of time on background checks. I have found that although in some areas this is wonderful but in certain arena a focus on that person set of principles that guides them in decision making is more important closely followed by their ability to learn rather than their knowledge. Doing this will help you to avoid bad business partnerships that are self-serving rather than collaborative. Returning back to work in order to support my husband after his illness I was once again placed on the battlefield of the worker's web. I was hired in as temporary employee who outlasted many of those coming in and out of the department when I discovered that my boss continually hired those coming in after me on several occasion. In the beginning, I was mortified. But I learned a valuable lesson. She could only see and chose those whom she felt closely aligned with her views. A quick overview of her desk, leadership and the department reminded me that I didn't fit in with those views because our views, leadership style and the manner in which she ran the department did not fit into my views therefore, I felt relieved that she didn't incorporated me into that mess. You can check one's leadership by how the department support or doesn't support each other. How do they act when the leadership is not present? Are they productive or is there always more work leftover than what has been achieved for the day. These principles allowed me to open the door to my own core beliefs in which I had developed over recent years. How do I want my company to run? What are our values, principles and core beliefs? What are the basis of these core values, principles and beliefs. Whenever you are developing an idea whether business or personal that you desire to enhance your ability, self-image or overall company strength these questions must be asked and answered prior to leaping forward. I have met a lot of people on my journey whom have had wonderful and solid ideas but because they failed to answer these questions in the early onset process of their idea they have watched their dreams pass them by. As I stated earlier, checking those around you in your inner core, answering the vital questions regarding your philosophies and belief system will assist you in overcoming some of the downfalls that entrepreneur's encounter. Take time to think about your beliefs and philosophies for your ideas. Meditate on the core principles in which you would like your business and personal image represents. Remember, this is your vision for your life. No one can say whether or not your vision is wrong nor can they say that your philosophy for living isn't correct. It is solely based upon those beliefs in which you have embraced. When developing your philosophy for your company it is developing a vision. The short, intermediate and long term vision. Too many times, people have written down their short and long term goals but no one seems to remember there has to be a bridge the intermediate goal that helps you cross over to the entity of that vision. When writing down your philosophy brainstorm the beginning, the middle and the end. Like any map your philosophy will guide you along the way as you begin the process of developing your vision.

Brain Mapping Your Philosophy

When brainstorming your philosophy I want you to think about who you are and who you desire to become. Sometimes these two need to be merged in order for your vision to become a reality. Ask the question if whether or not you need to educate yourself further on your business or personal goal. What do you hope to accomplish. All of these concepts goes into developing your philosophy. Your vision is more than just words. They will become your marker for how you live your life as well as how you develop your career, education or business. Everything you do will reflect upon your present ability to self-motivate yourself to keep moving forward towards your vision. I cannot tell you how many times an idea has come to my mind and as I tried to build it I watched it fall apart. There were many factors but one of those contributing factors was my inability to truly understand how important it was for me to develop my philosophy not based upon what the bank, business administrator and financier wanted to hear, but rather truly on what I believed and stood for in every aspect. This is the secret to achieving your dreams. When we take away what contradicts whom we truly desire and the soul of our being we then set ourselves up for the eventual downfall of our own dreams. In my opinion what set the mega giants of this world apart from all the rest of us who have dreams and those who have made their dreams come true is a small component which is called Truth. This is the nature of who you are. Your abilities and what you seek to accomplish will manifest itself regardless. Truth and destiny are intertwined. When these two intersect you will find yourself unstoppable. While working for a restaurant, I met a young man who was quite successful at his trade. In fact, he was dropping money for his friends as well as for the waitresses. When I asked him what he did for a living he said simply I provide my customers with excellent customer service and quality products. I meet the demands through the product I deliver. Again, I asked what business is that? Ma'am I am a drug dealer. I was stunned and laughed for a moment thinking he was joking around. I mean who would really just tell a stranger something like that, Right? I know you don't believe me but that's what I do. So, I responded, if that is true then why would you tell me that do I look like someone who would be impress by that statement. No, he responded. Listen, I have learned if you are going to be in any type of business including this one you must face the truth about who you are, once you accept that then you can move forward putting everything into developing yourself your image and your enterprise, that's how you become successful. Simply, by incorporating a true representation of yourself. That's what makes me one of the most successful dealers in this area. My response. What if you get busted and go to jail? Well that is part of my image and my enterprise I embrace it once I am completed with my term I simply resume as head of my business. So your business doesn't stop. No! not at all. I take care of my employees so they can run it while I am away and that's that. Although I didn't agree with his business, I do believe in his method. For anyone whom desire to achieve something you must first love, embrace and be comfortable with that image. This is why it is essential you develop a philosophy that represents you at the core. This will reflect through you when you are dealing with customers, or a boss or those who surround you in every arena of your life. So in the course of developing my business this time around I had to do something different. There was a reason I kept failing and this was one of those essential factors that I had to deal with in order to successfully launch a business in which no one could destroy. I had to get to a point where my true nature and what I love came through. So when I began this part of the journey I asked myself.

What did I want my products to stand for? This would play a valuable part in how my products were developed and where I bought my products. For example, did I believe selling lingerie was bad, evil or part of our daily lives and what kind would I sell in our store? The answers to these questions would reflect in my product choices and the clientele in which I wanted to serve. When I utilized this train of thought on my core values it fell into my beliefs on family and marriage. Did I think it was okay for Christian women to be sexy and naughty with their husband or was it shameful. Most importantly could we do it with taste. We sure can. This pattern of thinking went into every aspect of our business and every product line we developed. Our views and philosophies are reflected in our product line. By the way, YES I do believe Christian women can be Hot and Sexy with their husband. The evidence; the marriage bed is undefiled. Every aspect of my business sprung forth from these questions. No matter what business you are in you must think about what are the end result, who are products intended for? Who are you writing your music for? Every business has a genre and that is determined by your philosophy.

The "Why Me Factor"

This is probably going to be my favorite section of this book next to "Getting in the Game." Why? I am so glad you asked. Everyone has had those "Why Me Days" in their lives. These are filled with hindrances, obstacles, demons and plagues. They will come from every direction. Whenever you are on your way to developing your passion, that vision no matter how long it took you to get to this stage something happens. I know. For years, I lived in the "Why Me Factor" which would be more accurately titled the "Why Me Factory." It is like someone is mass producing hindrances, obstacles and stumbling blocks to keep you from reaching your dreams. It comes in the form of past mistakes, finances, deaths in family, illnesses, loss of work, enemies in the camp and other challenging roads. They always seem to come at the most inappropriate time. Just when you are about to open the door to your dreams something pulls you out of reach of the doorknob. In this chapter, we are going to deal with these issues. These factors can be the difference between you achieving your dreams or watching them disappear. Returning back to work was a real eye opener for me. Daily, I would listen to individuals have their gripe session about their jobs, how they really wanted to do this or that. If I only had just a few more credits to graduate and then I could have, but then this happened. I have only met one person who in my lifetime of working has said to me this is what I was made for there is nothing else I would want to do. No matter how hard this job can be, no matter how the people sometimes wreck my nerves I know this is what I was made to do and I love my job, I have everything I want. It was shocking. When I watched her over the next few months. I discovered this person is living her true self. She has aspired to do this and she is successful because she has achieved her goal for herself. It wasn't based upon anyone else. She didn't care if everyone thought she should have done but rather she did what made her happy. Daily she would come in excited about her job. No matter how many days she worked, she was happy. No complaints. She achieved her dream. So I wanted to investigate further. Why is she so darn happy about this factory job. Why was she successful while the rest of us whined and boo woo'd about our lives. How did she achieve this event in her life. Well, she pushed through. She didn't let anything, anyone or any situation stop her. She stop blaming everyone, everything and every situation for what she could not achieve. Instead she realized the only one to blame was herself. Because, of the excuses we allow ourselves to have in order to bow out of our dreams gracefully. For anyone to say to themselves, I have bowed out gracefully, it was a great feeling to just experience it and let it go is beyond shame itself. We as visionaries must learn to confront, execute and develop a plan for life's uh oh's! because they will come. Expectation of those situations will assist you in being prepared to motivate yourself to keep moving forward towards the goal. In this chapter, we will discuss this very principle. Though we can never be prepared for every situation life hands us we can at least be prepared to

cut through the runaway vines that have kept the door out of
reach.

Excuse Me While I Break Down an Obstacle

Yes, that's right! We have to sometimes put something on pause while we deal with a situation. Remember it is on pause, so you must get back to it quickly. When my husband got sick, I had to put a lot of things on pause. After a while, I just didn't go back and push the green button. This would happen time and time again. I would be developing an idea and just as it was about to break open it would happen the "Why Me Factor." Something or someone would hinder me from going forth. I would just come crashing down. Any obstacles or hindrance to my vision and I took it as sign that this wasn't for me. Going back to school, the finances fell through and I just quit. I was delivering food and when I didn't' get enough orders I quit. An argument would happen and the business was done. Somehow, I had to get pass those hindrances in my life. What is keeping you from the door? Well, patterns. Life has a pattern of obstacles in which move in a direction that opposes your current course. These patterns will dish out hardship in the fashion in which you have allowed your life to mirror. In other words, how you live will dictate the patterns of hardship that is given to you. When you begin to move in a different set of rules for your life the pattern will change. That pattern is based upon your thoughts about yourself. Remember, how you think of yourself will be revealed through your business, personal and financial modality of your life. No obstacle in the universe is randomly given to anyone but rather it is set in motion by your own set of rules in which you have governed yourself. I am firm believer that poverty is a state of mind. No one came make anyone poor or rich. You are not born into poverty but rather into a lost vision. Someone, allow their rules to dictate the hardship in which they have encountered that played a part in their own financial downfall. No one different. The richer and the poorer is due to an inner manifestation of beliefs that have developed over time. You have drop your vision somewhere along the way. You have stopped contributing to your dreams and it began to starve. Something or someone has tricked you into believing that you aren't worth the effort and you fell for it hook line and sinker. When these obstacles arise just excuse yourself from the table but not from your dreams. That is the mistake so many of us make. After talking to hundreds of people I have discovered three obstacles that have been detrimental to a dream being manifested. These three obstacles have killed a dream, buried a vision and eulogized an entire life.

The first obstacle and the easiest one is obvious. However, it has two parts to it's poison. The first obstacle is finances. Many of us await a windfall of finances whether from our income taxes or a loan. Let's face it! How many of us heard of a credit report in our generation before we were 12 years of age, how about 20 years? Nope, well that was the kicker. The score that killed a dream. Because many of us did not understand nor did we have knowledge of credit our dreams have went out the door because you need money to make money. The second part of this poison is waiting for someone to assist you. We partner up but never go any further. We talk but no one has the money. We dream but our credit score crushes our hope. Finances and partnerships go hand in hand. You believe someone is for you but they are really against. Lack of finances as we live paycheck to paycheck takes away our hope in a better tomorrow. The second obstacles is belief. For some of us a dream is just that a dream. No matter how much we want we have just decided that it was fun while it lasted but it takes too much time, money and effort to complete the dream and without the first obstacle there can be no dream. But, it really sounds good when we are sitting on the porch. Hmmm! Finally, the third obstacle which I find to be the saddest of them all. It encompasses many factors including environment. Even though the first two obstacles are pretty bad nothing compares to the third factor in the death of a dream. It will take work to overcome this particular step to achieving your dream yet so many are unwilling. It has taken the breath out of many souls. Once upon a time, it did the same thing to me. This obstacle is so cold that you will believe death has arrived and you will willing jump on the coach to take you to your new home. This obstacle is…… Self-Destruction through Mutilation. WHAT! Let me explain. I am an expert in this arena. You see, Once upon a time in a far away land.. just kidding. No I haven't gone schizophrenic on you just yet. But this is reality. Self-Destruction through mutilation is when you are the enemy in the camp. You work very hard to defeat yourself. So many individuals with a great idea will smash their own dreams before they get out of the gate. We utilize the rational factor to make or break ourselves. For example; have you ever heard someone say "I have this great idea that I am working on and I am ready to launch it directly following that sentence is I am scared. I mean you know what I mean. My friend or family member is doing this business and I have an opportunity to take it on but what happens if I fail. Right now, I have a good job with benefits. I can't lose that on my idea. Let me ask you this what is the worst that could happen? You already know the answer to that question. Now let me ask you the real question what is the best case scenario? You make it! Wow! But how will you ever know if you will cross over the enemy lines an actually make it to the goal line. No one who has ever made it across the line did it without some type of fear. There is always the devil on the shoulder ready to take you down security lane. He is like the real estate agent selling you the house that is out of your price range. Have you ever notice that when a sales person takes you on the tour of a house or a vehicle they take you through the best case most wonderful path of star line homes and cars first. Hoping one of them will catch your eyes and seize the greedy demon in all of us. The enemy will lock you down into a sale that you cannot afford so you will be indebted to the securities that have allotted you the opportunity to purchase such luxuries. However, luxuries don't amount to much if you are not free to dream. I remember talking with a friend of mines years ago. We were discussing this very thing about leaping forward and seizing our passion. Yet five years later we were having the same conversation. I began to wonder why were we having this same conversation when neither of us took the dream deal the last time. Fear! It was simple. We didn't want to be embarrassed, ashamed and most of all disappointed. We didn't want to have the conversation with ourselves. The one that says you tried and failed and now you have no other options. No more dreams. That was it. Game Over. Many of us spend our time in that mode of thinking all the time. We look to those around us to make a decision that validates our reasoning as to why we will not succeed. We can't because. Our family, children, spouse and employers rely upon us to be sensible. Well wake up dreaming is not sensible. There is no rhyme or reason to dreams that are outside the box. If you want to run the company you are currently working for then you will have to make a decision to complete what is necessary to achieve it. You must run the race until you reach the goal. Take the necessary courses, learn the impossible. Factoring in all the reason that could stop you then eliminate them before you get to the gate. This is how champions are made. No one is born a genius or a champion. They are made through determination, self-promotion and flat out guts. Yes, some of us have the genius gene and other's the champion is in the DNA. But the truth is if they don't activate what is in their DNA construct they will never make it out the gate. The difference is the absence of self-multilation. The ability to knock down the demon on the shoulder and take flight on their dreams. Imagine where we would be if the Wright Brothers had tried and failed. If they had walked away. Neither brother never said fear had escaped them. They just kept trying until one day their dream took flight. In the old days, I remember elders saying you can be anything you want to be if you set your mind to it. Back then, for African American it was a far stretch. I think every child was told they could be president of the United States of America. One of them was right. It took many years of obstacles, fear, fight and flight. It took thousands of individuals willing to sacrifice for the dream to take shape in President Barak Obama. I remember the 2008 election very clearly. It is the one election I will never forget as African Americans who had spent their lives as butlers, maids and laborer saw their dreams take flight. We had reached the promise land, crossed the goal line. For them, their sacrifice had finally been realized in President Barak Obama. In their lifetime, the dream was realized for every African American. It is shear determination that makes the difference between success and failure. It's the ability to never take no from yourself that launches you across the mine fields. This is what heroes are made of, many will tell you I don't know what came over me but I knew it was between me and death and I made the decision that **death and fear would not win today.** Can you imagine what that feels like, the pure adrenaline of belief that casts a shadow over your fear paralyzing it in such a way that it cannot interfere with your determination. That what it takes to start a business. That what it takes to achieve that promotion. That is what it takes to make the grade to become the champion in your own life. We are the example for our own achievements. We will right the legacy that begins a new chapter in our lives. Let me tell you once you have done it once, you will and can do it again. It's like an addiction once you achieve that superior high you will never want to let it go. You must have it again. Nothing will interfere in your dream war to succeed ever again. When I talk to my children, I tell them all the time. Write your own story. Don't let me or anyone else narrate what you can and cannot do. You are the author of your dreams. The enemy can't have it because he doesn't know what you are about to write and even if he did at a moments notice you can erase that journey and take a new path. That what it means to author your life. To take a leap into the field of dreams that is your destiny. So many of us lose that will or ability to know who you are. To decide and discover what is your passion. You need to find out because that is difference between you reaching your life's passion. This is who we are. I remember, my husband's aunt had passed away. She was a wonderful woman. But I kept thinking did she achieve all that she was purposed to do in her life. While sitting their amongst those who I really didn't know. I was surrounded by these young dreamers looking forward to their dreams. At that moment I thought my time had passed. I was attending my own funeral. I was burying my dreams. I had stopped exploring. After so many attempts I had decided I didn't make it because my time. My purposed passion was no longer attainable. But then, I had to go back to work. At that moment, I decided, if I can invest in someone else's dream. Let me explain this to you clearly. When you work for another company you are participating in someone else's dream. It is their dream be actualized. Every employee that wals the halls is someone else's dream being realized. This person walked through their fear. They removed the obstacles that would hinder them from succeeding. Fear and death go hand in hand. No realizing your dreams can leave you bitter, hurt and in an emotional war within yourself daily. It is why you go to work with such discontent. We drink, we do whatever we need to do to get to that job we numb the pain. You need to make a decision to change how you operate in fear. You are responsible for who you surround yourself with. Change your perspective take a different road. Stop driving down the same road to failure and take detour in your own life to get to your dream. There are people you may have around you that you need to get away from there are situation that you will have to walk away from. So many of us live in a constant continuum of loss because we have aborted our dreams. We walk around hammering other people down. We spend time in other people's past along with ourselves. We look at all of our failures and we record them in our mind. The mind is where we filter everything. We tell our minds that we are stupid, that we are not good enough. That we are a criminal, no one will believe you. We will knock our own self down in order to bring others down with us. But you have to learn how to box with the devil on a daily basis. You see it is your job to fight the war that is within you. That is where you will find your true worth, your true passion. You must push past the hang up moment. Sometimes no! let me change that most of the time when you are moving towards your dream. You will find yourselves achieving just enough but then you will walk away. Because something happens. The pain of fear and death. The stench of contentment and comfort will rise up and you will have to walk through it without a gas mask. You have to learn how to build a bigger bridge. It took me a long time to walk past my own stench in order for me to reach my dream. I had to learn to believe in that inner voice that kept telling me that I was intelligent, gifted and passionate. That I had the ability within me to make it. It was for me. I was created to do this dream. There is no one else in the world that can achieve this but me. There is nothing else that I was made to do with my life. No matter what anyone else believed, said. No one could see. Only I could see pass the thick clouds in my head. The brain is a atenna that will send the negative or the positive throughout your entire life. If you tell yourself you can't that it is impossible then you are filtering that information through your system. Your nervous system because paralyzed, your mind begins to detoriate, your emotions begins to take over causing you to feel angry, bitter and selfish. It is up to you to change the direction of your path. To understand that when the coals are hot on the ground it can either stop you or you can walk over it. It is up to you. I have watched what failure can do to someone's mind and body. They blame anything and everyone. The live in constant hatefulness. Don't respond. Instead change how those words are played in your mind. You have to make a decision that you want more fruit. If you tree isn't producing the right fruit root it out and plant a new tree in order to produce the fruits that you desire. There is more than just a few cherries. Gardening has taught me a lot. When a seed didn't take root. I would pluck it out. But then, I would see that deep down in the soil that seed is trying to take root. So instead of plucking it out I put it in new ground. A soil that is conducive to the seeds success. That is what we must do in our own lives. When a seed that we have planted isn't producing the right fruit or it isn't taking root at all. It doesn't mean you have a bad seed just that you need to move it to new ground. That it is why it is important to change your atmosphere. To change your environment and those things around you that is not agreeable with your success or growth. I have watch when you take a harden criminal and move him into unfamiliar territory he learns to adapt to the new grounds. No matter how much they want to resort to their old ways the conditions around them make it hard for them to produce those seeds. Then there are those seeds that no matter how tough the ground they will take root. They will not be plucked out. They will remove every stone and pebble in it's way. That's the seed that will produce the most fruit. One day, I saw this sign that said "impossible" Suddenly, my brain my perception saw the words "I AM POSSIBLE" WOW! When I began to acknowledge who I AM, when I decided no matter how hard it gets I AM POSSIBLE! What a realization. That is when I knew that I had began to change my perception on negativity. I had taken a bite out of fear and death. I would not let death and fear seize me. I knew what was within myself. I had went through my own personal inner war and fought my own enemy. I knew that my time had not passed but had developed. It had motivated me to move pass my fears, pass the hardship and negative environment. I had embraced my fear and used it as a tool to achieve my passion. You can because you are POSSIBLE! Tell yourself "I AM POSSIBLE." This is moment to ask yourself ARE YOU POSSIBLE? How do you feel about your life right now?

Let's Review

1. What does it mean to develop your philosophy?
2. Why is developing your philosophy is important?
3. Do you need to change your philosophy about yourself?
4. What fears have stopped you from developing your passion?

Staging Your Production

Many of us call this stage our goal-setting section. I call it staging your production. When I was writing a play for the church. I realized that the script was only part of the play. But the real work was staging the production. While writing the play it was staging the production that took more time. Writing the play was just a small part of the production. I had to figure out how I wanted to present this program. I had to stage the moments within the play. Every emotion had to be staged just right in order to truly reveal the essence or passion of the play. Staging your production for success is essential in developing your passion. It was up to you to figure out what you need to do in order to make this production a reality. Many dreams are not reachable because they have been told that they can't. That it is not possible. When you are writing the play for your life stage the production. What is going on behind the scenes. That means you must, let me repeat you must control what is going on behind the scene. Wht is going on in your mind. What does your stage look like in your life. Look at the characters, the voices in the script what is their tone. Then you tell yourself I can't make the audience feel what I am writing. Of course you can. It all about how you set the stage. How you dress, the language. What is on your stage. One thing I learned about putting together a play is this. Nothing you need is in the closet but rather it must be created. So you need to create the materials and props needed to produce the production of your life. Find out what will it take for you to achieve the dream that you have in your heart. There is a number in your heart in the production of your life. How much does it take. What needs to happen in this production for you to know that you have achieved the passion that you have set for yourself. I had to take a look at that in my life. On my stage was naysayers, the characters were acting out my failures. They were not on the script I had written for myself. When I looked at my life the production wasn't up to my standards. I had to change my production if I wanted to succeed. At this point in my life, I was tired of everyone devaluating who I am. Who I knew I was inside of me. But I began to play to the tune of everyone else's production. I had to reset the stage. Part of that was rewriting my script to eliminate what I began to believe about myself regardless of what I believed in my heart. While staging your production you have to find those individuals that will help me to fight the battle within myself. I leaned heavily upon the negative in my life. My mind had to revamp or more accurately resurrect the I AM in my life. One of my favorite scriptures in the bible is the conversation between Moses and God. Moses tried vehemently to lean on his negative. I can't speak clearly, I am not a part of them, I lived apart. Why would they listen to me. Finally, Moses wanted to lay it all on God. They won't know who I am talking about, So who do I say that has come before me. How will they know it is their God. He said simply, Tell them I AM has sent you. I began to write my script for my life around this script. **I AM and fill in the blanks**. I AM successful. I AM possible because God said I AM! This is when you learn that life is going to take a drastic change. The production is about to take a different direction. I had to learn how to continuously rewrite and edit the script regularly. You must encourage yourself because no one and let me tell you there will be few that will be in your corner to pull you out of the quicksand every time you step forward. Remember **the negative will never go away**. You talk to anyone who is successful right now and they will tell you even today negative thoughts have come across the screen in my mind. But today, I decided that I wasn't going to accept that script. At this moment you have to set the stage for our production. Clearing out the mind, sweeping out the heart and moving your body towards that dream. **No success can be achieved without clearing and re-creating the atmosphere and environment in your life.** Another part of my production that I have implanted into my script is learning to walk through the storms of life. So many people say when the storm hits stand in it.. No way am I going to stand in the middle of tornado. I am going to fight my way out of it because I want to live. Standing in the storm will kill you faster than finding a way through it. I remember a story during the Katrina storm when emergency teams had bunkered down to receive distress calls only to discover they would be the one in distress they didn't stand in the storm but rather they shot their way through the storm. They put bullets in the door in order to get out and walk, swim and float through it. That's what we have to do. Your philosophy about how to handle the storms in your production. This is where it counts. When you begin to develop your passion your philosophy has to change. This will set the stage in your production. **Nothing comes to bear fruit unless you begin to change the philosophy in your dream map.** I didn't want to just live , to survive. I am a known survivor of many things. I had to ask myself what in my mind made it so that I could work through the production that society had set forth for me. I had to overcome some things that should have sat me down, giving me the excuse to be less than. I realized that I didn't let the script of life and environment dictate who I AM. I had pushed myself beyond what I thought I could handle. When I got in the ring of life it hammered me, beat me down, it punched me and knocked me out more than once. I went through hundreds of rounds before I decided to pick myself up off the mat and learn to punch life back in the face. No longer was I going to be knocked down on my own stage. I love Mohammed Ali even though I am not a fan of boxing. He would get in the ring and tell his opponents you are fighting against the GREATEST. Believe it or not that statement knocked them down in the ring before Ali ever got on the mat. When you tell fear and death that I AM THE GREATEST because I AM. It has to flee, it can't stand before the presence of the I AM in you. When you are staging your production Part of setting the stage of your production pulling out the stops. Getting all the items necessary to produce this play. When I was putting together this play everything about it said it wasn't going to work. We didn't have a stage. WE had no costumes. So I had to get into the closet and pull out the fabrics in my dusty old garage with no sewing experience. I began to create the costumes for every character in the play. Every character was carefully thought out therefore every costume reflected every character. I had to step out and pull out and draw into myself regardless of what I didn't have. It was hard. But I had to put this production into motion. It was my business to make this happen. I say to you right now that no matter how hard it's get even when you don't see it's there. You must set the stage for yourself. You cannot allow the production of your life to fall apart. They is more to life than just substituting. Don't stop the production because you are short a few dollars or those you are supposed to help you produce the play have backed out. It is your passion, your dream, your moment to shine. You have more than 15 minutes of flame and fame in your life. Take every obstacle and embrace them. There is nothing you cannot achieve. It is up to you to challenge yourself and inserting within yourself the speech of a lifetime. It is your time. This is your production and you have the pen that can change your life. **There is nothing in your presence that says you cannot achieve in the future.** If you can start to take the first step no matter how big the anchor of fear is in your life you have the pencil and the eraser. You can erase it and re-write the production of your life. I AM POSSIBLE, then write it down. The production of your life may have started out with you being the last one on the list, the one that no one believed in, the one that didn't' get the award, you might be the one without the ability to count but you can put together something so great that it amazes others. Let no one tell you what isn't but rather surround yourself with those who believe that nothing equals nothing but greatness. Trust yourself , trust the script that will forever be the production of your life. You might know how it going to come to bear fruit but it will happen. I am a firm believer in no matter where you come from, no matter what you have been through no matter what road or how harsh that road may be you can make it through. You can cross over to the promise land designed just for you. When I think about he Isrealites who had to walk around that desert for 40 years talk about failure. But if they had only looked across they would have seen that the promise land was just across the border. But you have to develop an appetite for what you want. So stage your production. What does that mean. Well it means you have to prepare yourself begin reading, writing and listening to those things that will pump you up motivate you those things that will help you set the stage for yourself. **You have to be ready and prepared to take the lead in your own production.** When the opportunity jump out at you guess what you will be ready to take the reigns and ride it all the way to the promise land. You can be the champion in your own story. But you can't do that unless you prepare yourself ahead of time. It is time for you to set the stage for your production. Take your gift and talents and move forward to achieve greatness in your own life. Learn how to put together your production by knowing who you are. What gifts and talents do you possess right now! Too many of us spend too much time trying to figure out how you are going to do it. That is not a factor. The main stage is built upon what do you want? Secondly, put determination un-moveable and unshakeable commitment to that dream and drive that passion into your future. What? You have the cowboy or cowgirl that will wrangle the gifts and talents within you into the gates ushering them into your passion. Third, take that passion and drive deeper into yourself. You cannot be content with where you are. You cannot be comfortable in your life. No one reaches for a dream if they are comfortable in your circumstances. You are where you are in your production because of a choice you made to stay comfortable. Science has proven that many of us do not use enough of their brain capacity. A genius pushes their brain beyond its current limitation. You have to make and resolve within yourself to push yourself beyond your current limitation. When there is nothing you can do but move forward that is where you will find your passion. When those question in your heart arise and feel that you don't have what it take. When you think you are not smart enough, rich enough or got nothing else. Pick yourself up and run the race anyhow. When your shoes fall apart run with your socks. When your socks lose its stitching run with your feet. Well, I was you a long time ago. Everyone said I wouldn't be nothing. You have to know what you can't see yet. That is the most difficult thing to get passed in your life. Removing the seen factors from the unseen. You can't base your life on what you see but rather on what you can't. Everyday it is your business to encourage, motivate and challenge yourself. Your business begins in your heart and mind. This is your day. That's right everyday belongs to you. When you begin to take that type of leap into your life you will develop and discover your passion. Daily speak to yourself. Change the music in your head. Play a new tunes. Again remember you are the I AM POSSIBLE in your own life. I remember sitting there saying to myself I don't have the money to make this business work. I don't have the partnership, the odds are against me. Then I realized that

if I contemplate on what I don't have then I will never have it. But if I move beyond what I don't have and focus on what I possess. One of my favorite movies is the scrooge. Why? Because I see this movie differently. I saw the ghost of past dreams that I did not fulfill. Then the ghost of present visions and dreams that were ready to bury itself. Then the ghost of future dreams that will never be realized because I refused to take action on my dreams. We have pushed the pause button on our dreams because we don't want to see the failure that lies ahead. You have to push replay on your vision. Stop pushing the pause button on your dreams. When you pause you stop living. Throw away your fake ID's and push the play button. It's time to take your foot off the brakes and let it go. It's time to drive forward. Your passion is right there bearing down inside your heart. You have to keep going no matter what it looks like. Your dreams have already tempted you and now it's time for you to taste what has been laid out before you. Stop trying to wait till you have everything in place. No one makes when they have everything in place but rather when they have some missing pieces that will fall into place when you get out there. You don't have the money? So ask yourself, what do you have to get the engine started? **What do you possess right now to make it happen?** Who do I need to remove from my life that are not benefiting you. It's the next chapter we will talk about developing your team players. You can't be with people on the same level as you. You can't be surrounded with people who are just getting there. You have to put together a team that is out of your range that how you will reach your goals. You can't sit with those who have not reach it yet. You can't be around those who are where you are right now. But instead take those people who you know have the bank account you desire. The one you has the position you desire. If you want to reach your potential then surround yourself with those people who have reach beyond your limitations and reach the goal.

Let's Review

1. **I AM and fill in the blanks**
2. **Remember the negative will never go away.**
3. **No success can be achieved without clearing and re-creating the atmosphere and environment in your life.**
4. **Nothing comes to bear fruit unless you begin to change the philosophy in your dream map**
5. **There is nothing in your presence that says you cannot achieve in the future.**
6. **You have to be ready and prepared to take the lead in your own production.**
7. **if I contemplate on what I don't have then I will never have it.**
8. **What do you possess right now to make it happen?**

The Affirmation for Success

1. I ready and study because I AM The Champion of my Dreams
2. I can because I AM Great
3. Nobody can steal my dream because it is MY VISION in which they do not have access
4. My success is in my hands, my mind and my heart
5. Everything I do will be Great because it is my destiny
6. My mind is my greatest asset
7. The gate to my success cannot be open except by my heart and passion
8. All negative words and action have and will be erased daily
9. I am the author of my dreams so I will write a new goal in my heart everyday
10. I AM the champion and the HERO of my own story
11. Daily my dreams and vision are being realized
12. The tools I need to be GREAT and live my passion is here right now.

Remember write your name on it this is your daily affirmation for success.

Set Apart

Think about this statement for a moment "set apart." You have been set apart to achieve something great. When you begin to set the stage for your production you will always most assuredly encounter the question **what set's you apart from others in your field?** I was sitting at the table with a group of friends whom had gather to sort of mastermind our goals. One of the outside members asked me what was my goal for my company. I explained to him it was to put the other company on its knees. SO he asked how are you planning on doing this? My response was simply it doesn't matter how it will be what set's me apart from my competition. This is important in any field. **What about you will set you apart?** No one think that to make a plan to set yourself apart. Part of your philosophy is documenting what sets you apart. I know we all remember the computer wars of the early 80's and nineties. But only two companies from the soup bowl of companies that were out there. Steve Jobs and Bill Gates both are in the same industry but both of them set themselves apart from the other. Neither is more successful than the other because not only did they set themselves apart but they also set their clients or consumers apart from the other. Whatever you are deciding to do with your life goals is what sets you apart. Why will those consumers leave another and come to you. What kind of service are you providing? How do your consumer feel when they purchase something from you whether it is a product or a service. What is the outcome? What does your competitor provide for their consumers that draws them back. Somehow they have created a habit forming buying strategy for their consumers? What habit forming buying strategy are you utilizing to produce a positive outcome for your customers. While creating the product or service what drew you to decide this was needed. Then ask yourself what catalyst will you place into your strategy that will break the bond between the previous buying strategy and yours. How do you feel when you receive this product or service. This is essential. An important factor is to sit down and figure out what is your 80/20 percentile. When you are developing what set's you apart determine which factors and tasks will give you the highest outcome for the minimum amount of effort. What set's you apart will become your marketing leverage. The leverage in marketing is the difference between you and your success. When we talk about leveraging many of us look at marketing as tell everyone about your business or promotion. The reality is marketing leverage is connecting with people. When you are able to connect with your customers then you are creating a marketing strategy that lasts. So many businesses fail because they can't get out the gate. The connect it with the lack of marketing skills or points of sales. However, when we learn that our business as an entrepreneur is to create a soul connection with your customers. You have as the leader is to create an atmosphere of desire for your customers. What do you have that they want? This is the first question you must ask about your product or service. People buy because you meet a need. There is something that they desire to have in their lives that only you have the ability to give them. That is the marketing behind the success of the fitness industry. Why are there so many fitness guru's and millions of people fall into their marketing. They BUY! BUY! BUY!

No matter how unsuccessful they are at following through on the fitness program. WHY! WHY! WHY! The reason is because they are meeting their needs. Their customers desire to be sexy, look good, have a beautiful body that attracts others. There is not one person in the world who is comfortable with the way their bodies look except the fitness industry. Have you ever noticed that every fitness expert walks around half dressed. They are attracting you to their business. You want what they have. That is marketing leverage. You want it and they can tell you how to get it! That is marketing leverage. They didn't have to create the desire because it was already there inside of their customers. All they did was develop a product around their customers desires. That is what makes millions of dollars. People want to achieve. They want to know it's possible to look great. Obtain happiness. They want something in their lives. You are there to fulfill that need. Whatever, you are trying to achieve you will discover once you have obtained it you will have the opportunity to live beyond your happiness. You are at the point in your life where change has to happen. You are missing something in your life. There is a need that has motivated you to do something about your life.

At the beginning of this book. We talked about where you start a business or gain a promotion or achieve your goals. It doesn't start with money. It begins in the mind. It begins with how you think about yourself. What do you need in order to transform your life? Your customers are in the same place. What made Oprah Winfrey successful wasn't that she was beautiful or extraordinary. But rather she tapped into people's need to discuss issues that weren't appropriate at the dinner table. Things you couldn't say out loud. At that time people couldn't say they were unhappy in their marriages. We as a human melting pot couldn't discuss the trials of life that scarred us on the inside. We were trained to hide it, fake it and pretend it never happened. Oprah Winfrey changed all of that for millions of Americans. What we couldn't deal with openly she made it possible for us to encounter publicly. You have to openly engage yourself daily. **Deal with your failures and learn from them what you didn't learn before you failed.** It is your responsibility to tap into your own passion and live it. Your story will help you to transform your life in a manner in which you will triumph over those things which have kept you from achieving. This leads me to our next point.

Developing Your Passion

Happiness is Taking A Risk

We have all taking a risk in something. Life is not without risks. Everything you have done means you have taking a risks in order to achieve. Every relationship is a risk, every job interview is a risk. No one knows if it will work out. But you were willing to take the risks in order to **find out what you are really capable of obtaining in life.** That is what it takes to be successful in anything in your life. Your life is a risk. Birthing a child is a risk. Birthing your business is a risk that many never attempt. So many would rather abort their vision than to take that risk of failure. In order to live the life you desire you will have to flip the switch in your brain from comfort to risk. We are wired to be comfortable, safe and secure. We do not like uncertainty. Boy! If we all could know ahead of time if we were going to be successful we would all be at the front of the line picking up our success ticket. So what is taking a risk? It is getting back up after you have failed. When I tell you failures was my first name, signature and last name, I mean that! But what I learned about business is that taking a risk is really is picking your face up off the ground and still have the guts to say open for business the next season. I began my business and it has evolved each and every time. I learned something every time I had failed. There is nothing wrong with failure when taking risk except when you don't learn how to improve your business on the next evolution. I had to learn to take my failures and pick myself off the floor. Most importantly, I had to learn how to slam the door on naysayers. That was really hard for me because I was the biggest naysayer in my business. Slamming the door on yourself is really hard. You have to figure out which side of the door are you going to stand on. Will you be on the right side of that door? Taking a risk means you are on the outside of that door because, nothing motivates you like the fear of being homeless. When you know there is nothing else but up you can get up and dust yourself off and make it work. When you are faced with a brick wall on your backside and nowhere in front you have to carve a path in order to find your way out of that cave. Insecurity goes right out the door. Failure doesn't cross your mind. Comfort is not an issue but rather survival. What the difference. What is happening in your mind. When it begins to tell you that there is no way out except for the path you make, the door you open. The only way to triumph over insecurity and fear of failure to take that risks in your life is to discover that there is only one option change your mindset. Dig your own path. Risk is everything is success. I have heard many people say to me that's great when you don't have any responsibilities. That is one of the first things I hear from people. My responsibilities keep me from taking a risk. Let me tell you; It was really hard for me to take that risks because of all of the responsibilities I had in my life. However, part of my failures was that I let my responsibilities dictate my level of commitment to building a business. I let my responsibilities take over my happiness. Millions of people are unhappy with life because of responsibilities. The truth is your responsibility first is to be successful. If you are successful then you feel confident which leads to you giving and sharing that confidence, success and happiness with others. It is infectious. When I am unhappy so is everyone else around me. I sit with people are dissatisfied with their lives. In fact, we have built entire religions from dissatisfaction in our lives. We need hope, faith something to keep us from stabbing ourselves in the eye on most days. But when you take the responsibility for your own life and say Hey! It's my life and I want to be happy. Then you will begin to take the necessary steps to develop your passion for life. You will begin to take the initiative to learn what you need to become the guru of your industry. This applies to every aspect of your life. You can transform your misery into a gold rush of success. Risk is becoming hungry which leads you to become willing to take a risk. One of the conditions for success that drives people is being uncomfortable. It means that misery has taken a leading role in your production. **You have to be willing and motivated to take a risk in your life that may not be comfortable.** Your responsibility becomes success, it becomes achievement. There is nothing more important at this point in your life than being the BEST man or woman you can be. When you are able to take the leading role in your production for happiness and success then you are able to lead others down the same path. Sometimes that means making a decision in your life that is uncomfortable or may lead you to insecurity. For example, a friend of mines had been married for years. She wasn't happy in her marriage but it worked. One day, her husband wanted a divorce. That particular situation had placed her in her own cave. She had to figure out what to do with her life. Up until that point, her life was her marriage. She worked, taking care of her responsibilities. Now she had to ask herself how will I make it on one income? Where will I live? That conversation in desperation led her to open her own bakery shop from within her apartment. That same woman now has her own bakery in town. She took a risk. That what we all must do in any situation. If you want to know what it means to be successful and how to achieve happiness the key term is risk. This doesn't mean that you just drop your responsibilities. Leave your spouse or walk away from your family. What it means that you have to learn how to motivate yourself to make some **sacrifices in order to meet your success.** Finding the gauge that will break your connection to the comfort of an American Dream that you are constantly chasing to one that you can embrace. It's up to you to decide what responsibilities can take a backseat. But don't let those responsibilities lead you to enslavement. There are those you have to take care of but make sure that you are embracing and incorporating those responsibilities into your dreams.

That's the difference. You don't leave your responsibilities but rather you incorporate those into your dreams for success. There is nothing more valuable that you can do for yourself than to embrace your responsibilities and incorporate them into your dreams. When you embrace and incorporate everyone and everything around your dreams you will find that everything in your environment will begin to fall into place. Everything and everyone in your environment will begin to contribute to the dream. There is nothing more empowering than having someone in your corner. Especially yourself. It will empower you to take risks in your life. It will allow you to give yourself permission to take those risks. Many of us don't believe that our minds don't listen unless we give ourselves and our brain permission to succeed. **Giving ourselves the permission to take a risk until doing so is automatic.** I was once told that it takes a moment to develop a habit and a lifetime to break it. In anything you desire it will take a lifetime to get yourself to the point where it is necessary to break the cycle of lack, suffering and misery. But once you have done it there will be no going back. Removing yourself from the comfort zone of that is your life right now to the life you desire takes will power and risk. There has to be enough fire in your pot to move you into action. Imagine if you told someone that there kitchen was on fire when really there is just a little grease popping on the stove. How fast will they move to put that fire out? They have been motivated to move into action. You need some fire in your passion to get you to take the risk into achieving and developing your passion for life and success. No one has ever been criticized for taking a risk and failing as they have for never doing anything about their passion. Stop talking and do something about your life. Take a Risk.

Let's Review

1. **Happiness is taking a risk**
2. **Don't let responsibilities steal your passion**
3. **Risk is becoming hungry enough to take the risk**
4. **You have to be willing and motivated to take a risk in your life that may not be comfortable.**
5. **make some sacrifices in order to meet your success.**

6. Give yourself permission to take risks in order to achieve

7. It is your responsibility to succeed so others can achieve

8. Let your failures be the lessons for your success.

9. Developing Your Passion is a risk

10. Know that there will always be obstacles when you take risks.

11. Hardship is the bridge to your dreams.

12. When all else fails dig another path to your dreams.

The Script to Success

After years of writing plays I discovered something about developing each script. The words were in my mind. Every character had its own voice in my head. I could hear everyone of them as I typed down what they were going do, how they were going to do and what they were going to say. It's amazing that when it comes to writing down someone else's destiny we are able to pump it out. Yet, when it comes to our own script for our lives we collapse in the midst of every scene in our lives. We all have a script that plays out in our lives and it is the one that everybody else has written down for us. We listen to every voice that has ever spoken a negative word but we delete all of the positive aspect of conversations that says you are beautiful, handsome, smart, gifted and capable of achieving anything. Instead what we hold onto is those negative scripts. In fact, we play them over and over again in our heads. We believe in every word and live it in every aspect of our lives. Let's face it, most of us don't succeed because of the script we have written for ourselves along with the exclamation marks that everyone else has included. Just like puppets on a stage we live every moment of it daily. We wake up go to work, eat what the commercials say is good and tasty. We punch into life and punch out. But there is something different that clicks in others who succeed. They don't listen to the negative scripts. It doesn't mean they don't hear them.   The difference is daily they delete the negative. They listen to the script delete the scenes that don't fit into their goals for the day and then move into the scripts that do fit into their daily goals. Who you have become is dictated much by your own beliefs and the scripts that you play in your mind. We have all heard this cliché "How man thinketh so is he." This is probably one of the most truest statements about mankind every written. We are how we think. If those thoughts gravitate towards the negative atmosphere we will never be able to move beyond that point in our belief. However, when we begin to consciously remove any negative statements that do not lend itself to motivating us towards our daily goals then any person can do the miraculous. In this book the miraculous is living your passion. Your script may say you are too old to go back to school. Maybe, it was the earlier statement of "I have too many responsibilities" I can't becomes I am scared. Whatever the script that is playing in your head you have to delete that statement. When you delete it replace it with a positive. There is room in your memory base for a new script. One of the most powerful things that I have done for myself was to acknowledge my fears as well as those conversations in which I have daily with myself that says, I can't, my past is holding me back, my responsibilities, track record whatever it is that is negative I have embraced it, acknowledge they are what they are statements but they are not who I am. These negative thoughts and conversations we have within ourselves will be the greatest battle we will ever fight. It is not those on the outside but the voices on the inside that will halt your dreams from becoming a reality unless you transform your mind. In other words, transform your thinking and you will transform your life. If I believe I am successful today then I will be however, if I believe the opposite so shall it be as well. The mind is a powerful tool. It can lend itself to be your saving grace or your worst nightmare. It can be the cause of your failures as well as your success. Learn daily how to converse within yourself. Wake up!

With encouraging words and statements that empower you to move into action. Challenge every negative statement with an empowering affirmation. Stay there until you begin to feel what you speak. Everyday when I have to go to work for someone else I empower myself to do something that helps me to achieve my goals for the day for my passion not just there's. I talk to myself constantly conversing and battling and casting down anything that isn't profitable for my success daily. When I go to work it's for me. It provides an atmosphere for me to learn and perfect my skills in business. It helps me to connect with potential customers. I am able to do market research as well as develop my passion and vision. One of my favorite scriptures and practices in which was written is found in the book of Philippians chapter 4 which states; "**Finally, brethren, whatever is true, whatever is honorable, whatever is right, whatever is pure, whatever is lovely, whatever is of good repute, if there is any excellence and if anything worthy of praise, dwell on these things.9The things you have learned and received and heard and seen in me, practice these things, and the God of peace will be with you.**" I wake up in the morning, go through my day and do everything in power to practice this statement as I seek to achieve my daily goals. He says, FINALLY! In other words, henceforth, from now on, get yourself together. Finally! You have realized that this is your script. You must practice it, dwell upon and discover it daily. He says, dwell upon anything that is true, anything that is good, motivating, encouraging, helpful anything that would move you into excellence, anything that is worth praising about yourself then dwell upon that script. Forget about what everyone else thinks about you, says about you. Make it your personal goal daily to say to yourself TODAY! Finally, I am going to dwell upon those things in my life that are beneficial to my success. Those things that encourage me to move forward today. I am going to challenge myself everyday to focus on those things about myself that are worthy of praise. It doesn't matter if yesterday was a day full of bad decisions. Today, is another day. This is where you will begin to develop your passion. There is a gateway in your soul that will lead you to learn how to motivate yourself. Remember those closest to you will be first one to gripe, moan and put you down. But it is up to you to rise up daily and dwell upon those things that are worthy of your time. You are responsible for what you take into your life. If somebody doesn't agree with your decision then they need to move on down the road. But, it is you who must battle the mind that is telling you that nothing is nothing and everything is everything. It's what you fill in on those lines that makes the difference in you achieving your goals daily. You are the judge that will determine if you have lived it today or not. You are the one that will pat yourself on the back when everyone else has a knife to it. It's up to you. Your script, Your pen it's time to change your life. You can transform your life simply by deleting those things which are not profitable and replacing it with those things that are beneficial. Ain't nothing wrong with erasing and starting all over again. Sometimes we have to start from the beginning in order to find our way out of the conversation that has given us nothing but grief. No matter how many times you have to go back to the board do it until the script fits into your life. Don't let life write your script.

Let's Review

1. Delete negative thoughts daily
2. Dwell upon those things which are praise worthy
3. Don't let others dictate how you are going to live
4. Don't let your words defeat you
5. Empower, Encourage and Motivate yourself early
6. Wake up with your mind set upon goodness
7. Don't let others interrupt your daily goals
8. Challenge yourself to writing positive statements about you daily
9. Your script, Your Life , Your Pen.. Write Something Good.

Getting in the Game

One of my favorite sports is football and bowling. Both of them takes focus. You cannot be half in or half out to win it. I have found that when I don't win it is because my head wasn't in the game the way it should have been. Oftentimes, I have asked myself, why didn't I do better in my life in every aspect. Why am I always choosing the wrong path? The answer is I wasn't in the game. I settled for whatever came my way because I didn't believe I could do it. Secondly, I didn't really want it. Third, I didn't deserve to have it. Whenever you are going to get into the game you have to have a strategy for how you plan on playing this game. What is your role on the field of dreams. Ask yourself what do I need to know before I get out on the field. You have to practice your strategy. Prove your statement to be true. You have to put together a team, an image, develop your strategy for success. You need to know what is your end game and how you plan on achieving that dream. There are many strategies to utilize to bringing a film to production or taking a losing team and transforming them into Super Bowl Sunday winners. There is a strategy to getting in the game. When you are developing your passion finding that strategy is imperative. I often reference scriptwriting because it takes a lot to bring a character full circle. First, brainstorming is on the table. This is when you begin dumping out every idea you have running across the field. Every character, scenes, the words and the backdrops. The reason you have to lay it all out there is so you can discern which ones fit together to make the full picture. Every strategy and thought do not compliment each other. Yet there are pieces in that vision that work together. It's like a kid, when you ask them what they want to become when they grow up. They will throw it all down. I want to be firefighter, a policeman, a model, a doctor and the list goes on and one. But once, they begin to find out who they are and discern between their passions and what sounds good they slowly begin to put those pieces together. This will go on for years as they find out what they are most passionate about. It doesn't mean they don't like the other but this is there passion and it fits with their goals and image for themselves. There overall picture. Once they have figure that out they begin to master what compliment their passion. As they go through school they put together the pieces that help them to develop their passion into a reality. They in turn, get in the game. Something happens to many of us when we hit a certain age. After about 26 years of age we begin to settle into life. We just happen to naturally go with the flow. Dreams become about surviving and making the grade. We lose that sense of grandeur in our minds. We no longer shoot high but we aim at what is feasible and reasonable in our lives at the time. We have turn away from dreaming or feeling passionate about the original vision in our lives. There are millions of people walking around unhappy because they have turned their backs on their dreams because they didn't get in the game. When you have a passion for something it up to you to get in the game. Whatever, your passion is begin defining it for your life. We walk off the field never finishing the game. Paul says in the bible, I am going to run the good race till I reach my goal, until I reach the finish line. How many of us don't even get in the lane. Learning how to get into the game can be difficult especially if you feel you have reached what society calls our primetime. Not our prime but primetime; the last leg of the race. Alright, you are asking what is the game and how to do I get into the game. Well there are many steps and based upon your passion and gauge for success will tell you what must be done. However, here are some basic principles for getting into the games. First, let's talk about your field. Anytime, a team is walking onto a field they look around. They need to know where is there goal line? How does the field feel to them? Who is their opponent and how will they beat them? So here goes; are you ready to walk onto your stage, your field? The first thing you need to do is to get to know your territory. What do you need to know about your surroundings, the field in which you plan on becoming a participant. You cannot get into the game if you don't know the rules for engagement. What does it take for you to become the best in the business? Is there any educational or licensing requirements in which you need to fulfill. Preparation is key to developing your passion. Find out who is the best in your industry and find out what they did to become the best in the business. Remember, we are aiming for the gold. We are going all in. Today, make a decision to find out who are the best in your industry. Write down their names and study them. Believe it or not they will become your best allies as well as your opponent. You need to have a strategy for defense and another to draw them closer. You need to discover what they have in order to get what you want. Knowing your opposition will help you to develop a strategy for your own success in the field. The first thing you will do is learn from them. Secondly, begin to study them. There is a difference. Learning is finding out about who they are and what they know. But, studying them takes determination and dedication. You will have to learn what makes them tick. How do they get up every morning. What is their rituals for providing their services or products to others. How do they receive their clientele. What places do they attend? Are there any conferences, resources or tolls they utilize in order to develop their model of success. That what it means to study. Discover what makes them good and why do others agree with that statement. Next, begin to apply some of those things to your strategy. For example, If Mr. X gets up daily and goes to a specific place for lunch find out why. Go have lunch there. Believe me there is a reason he is dining there. It's the environment. People flock to their own images, environment and mimic those rituals daily. This may be where networking goes on for your particular field. Write down those strategies in which they have turned into success. Learn and study them. Third, change your environment. Success follows success. Part of getting into the game is for you to get involved in developing your passion. There is nothing like a player sitting on the side lines. How long have you been sitting on the sidelines of your dreams. How long have you been watching your life from the sidebars. Those who are successful in your field is because they decided to get involved in the life. They prepared themselves. They reached a point where watching and complaining from the side lines is not enough. Somewhere along the line they asked themselves, how do I get in the game? Why is everyone else playing on the field of success but I continue to sit on the sideline. It's up to you decide if you are going to get involved in your vision for your life. Everyone may see the greatness. Your life may look like that of someone who can be successful but if you don't get involved in the game. There is no winner that can play the game if He/she is not playing the game. What if you never got out of bed daily. How would your body react. The fact is if you are not involved in your field, if you are not playing and learning the game you cannot win. One of the things coaches do is to help their team members to set goals for the game. You got to set goals everyday. You have to plan daily. Write down what your goals are for learning and studying every aspect of your field. You have to saturate yourself in your dreams. Everything you do must be designed to put you in the game to win. You have to stop waiting for scoreboard to light up on your behalf. It's up to you to decide what that scoreboard is going to represent for you. You have to look around your environment and begin to develop your team. When you gain wisdom in your game by studying and learning about your vision then you can really get into the game. No one can walk onto the field without knowing what game they are play. Can imagine a stock car driver pulling his car on a field filled with football players. Unless he is singing the national anthem he is out of place. It's up to you to know what is your game plan. What field are you going to play. When you begin to learn the game, practice the game and apply those principles to your passion in your life you will begin to daily pursue your passion. When you are on the field in the game you will see the difference in how your life responds to your action. How your mind respond to the strategy. There will be an automatic transformation in your environment. There will be a change in your conversation. How you discern and live will begin to change and impact your atmosphere. I always know what I am going to focus on that day. Before you can play the game you must know the game. Increase your knowledge in your field. Achieve through knowledge. Before you plant know what ground you are putting your seed. Learn, Study, Apply and participate in the game.

Let's Review

1. Are you in the game?
2. Do you have a strategy for the game you plan on playing
3. Are you ready to participate in your passion
4. Study others in your field
5. Learn everything about your passion
6. What do you need to fulfill your dream

ACTION!

It's time for you to walk into your season. The ground has been fertilized. You have removed and embraced every fear. You have acknowledged that obstacles, hardship and fear will arise. But you have determined that you will walk through the storm and not allow it to beat you down. You have decided to learn how to do it. You have study the greatest in your field. Now it's time for the engagement. It's time for you to dress the part. Your image, your style, your time. You cannot sit back and learn it, study it and apply it and never take action on your passion. If you plan on developing your passion you got to know first of all that it is worth everything you have gone through. Everything you will endure. Go back to your philosophy that lit the flame in your heart. Now begin putting everything you have learned in this book and from others. You have to put it into action. Never give up. Never allow someone to enslave your mind. Remember whenever you are punching someone else's clock you are walking in their passion, their dreams. But when you utilize that to strike a flame in your soul. When your vision ignites a passion that will not be distinguished it's up to you. It's up to you to step into that role. Define and refine the script for your life. There isn't anything you cannot have nor obtain unless you have made a decision to rob yourself of your own vision. Confront every issue and obstacle with a plan to take hold. Cast down every imagination that is not beneficial in your life. Believe me when I tell you reaching for your dreams can be difficult. But I have a plan that there is a door to the other side that I can open. I can find it. If the door is closed I will dig a path to my dreams. There is nothing more than achieving your dream. Train yourself to be successs and become success. Work on your mind daily. Your success is dependent upon your level of commitment to yourself. Re-scripting every aspect of your conversation. Ask yourself, how can I do what I want to do by improving what has already been done? Prepare those around you to participate in the dream. Set goals daily. Many of us set life goals but we don't reach those goals because we haven't set goals daily to move ourselves towards our passion. Those goals will be the fuel to help you achieve the vision you have set for yourself. Begin to speak to yourself every morning. Encouraging and empowering yourself that you can do it. Don't believe the lie. Don't buy into the lie that life tells you. There is more and life is broader than you can ever imagine. You can transform your life no matter where you came from. It doesn't matter what your past says you are. It cannot make you react and live it unless you perform it. No that impossible is really the statement that I AM.. Developing and achieving your passion is not rational. If you don't love what you do, if you don't have a passion for what you are doing you will quit. It all begins with passion. When fears sets in ask yourself this question. "If today was the last day of your life; what would you like to accomplish?" That is your passion. That's the thing you love more than anything. Many of us will say my family, this or that. But what would you have liked to accomplished in your life. Now ask yourself, if you have 12 days to live a little more time than the last day. What would you have like to accomplish and what would you do to get it done? How will you achieve it? Discover your next step. Every time you do something ask yourself does this contribute to your dreams. Success is built upon those who are prepared to meet opportunity at the door. If you are not dressed, prepared and plan to meet opportunity then you will fail. We have all made mistakes and things we wish you hadn't done. Things we wish hadn't happen to us. Things we wish we hadn't done to others. But don't let it imprison you, don't let it sentence you to a life of misery. That is a deception. You have to continuously remind yourself that your past is not who you are it is only the tool that has motivated you transform your life. It is the lift that encouraged you to look deep inside of yourself and step into your season. You have to go forward. Don't worry about what everyone else is doing but only what you are doing. They cannot help you get there. You have to put into your life everything you can. Put everything you can into your dream. Sometimes you might be broke that moment but you that doesn't mean you will be broke tomorrow, or tonight, or next week. It's up to you to place within yourself. If you make a decision, determine that this is not your life it is only a temporary delay in pay then you will put everything into your business. I personally, had to believe in this season that nothing was going to stop me. I had laid down many times, I had quit and thrown in the towel. I didn't think I could make but then one day. I decided no matter what my passion must be fulfilled. I refused to die without contributing to my life. So I began to develop my passion. I learned never to take no for answer. It just means right now it's not time. You have to create the atmosphere, to develop your passion. Stop wandering in the desert of life. You have to work hard. Even when the pain comes push through it. Think about what you have sacrificed this far. Complete what you have started this is one of those obstacles you will have to overcome. Challenge yourself. Ask yourself; how can you be better? This goes beyond just thinking and growing wealth. It's about being able to be flexible in adjusting your plan . Constantly contribute to your goals daily. Challenge yourself to constantly grow, plan, prepare and apply what you have learned to your passion.

Laying out the Red Carpet

Becoming successful is based upon the extreme circumstances that have motivated you to go beyond mediocre to success. When you strive to live beyond what you can see then you will be able to touch your dream. Research has shown that those who know how to see past the obstacles in their life then you are able to become the person you desire to become. For anyone, you need to define your identity. Know who you are. Activate that identity in your life. Start with your passion and purpose. Who you are is about establishing the foundation. No business begins with funds. Money doesn't start a business. Money can't give you passion. No matter what happened in your past that has placed fear in your life remember it cannot and does not have to be your present. If your past isn't your present then it has no place in your future. Create an environment that is conducive to encouraging you in every aspect your life. In my life, the government doesn't expect you to make it. The bank doesn't want you to make it. Your past doesn't want you to make it. The question is do you expect to make it. I spent a large portion of my life holding onto my past. Traumatic events in my life had intimidated me to lay down my own life. I desired and my passion at one point was to end my life. I had to change my identity. I had to let go of my past. I wanted to stop living. I had believed life was just what it is. I had to decide to change the game in my life. I ask myself, what do I need to do to change the statistics in my life. Do not accept what you see. Write your own story in for your life. Portion of your life have been blindly accepted. Do you really want success in your life? Then know that there is no shortcuts, no quick tricks to becoming successful. It takes go old fashioned hard work and a belief in yourself to succeed. Being willing to sacrifice and build is something you will have to do everyday. Daily you have to invest in yourself. We tend to invest in everything else but ourselves. If you are not willing to invest time, money and sleep into yourself then don't expect anyone else to invest in you. It's up to you to invest in your life. You cannot become successful if you are not able to take the time to set goals, to motivate and take initiative to achieve your dreams. Setting the goals daily to make my dreams a reality was difficult. If you count up how much time you have wasted in a day. In a year there are about 525, 950 minutes in a year. How many of those minutes have you invested into your passion. Into your dreams. Most of us spend approximately 10,500 to 12,480 minutes every year at work. We spend about 8, 750 hours sleeping annually. What are you doing for the remaining 504,000 minutes annually? That's how much time you have to invest in your passion. When we put it into perspective we really have plenty of time to study, learn and invest in your passion. I have learned to invest my time into what I love. Most of us don't spend any time on what we claim to love. You have approximately 25,000 hours to spend with those you love and still have plenty of time to spend on your business. So time cannot be an excuse as to why you are not successful. You have plenty of time to invest in developing your business brand. To learn and study from others who have already become successful. There is plenty of time for playtime and investment time. There is nothing stopping you but fear. Those dreaded obstacles that seem to come up right when you get ready to start up. But remember a startup is a set up and an opportunity to succeed. It's an opportunity for you to strive for something better. When failure comes learn what you need to do in order to do it better next time. Don't ever stay down. Re-visit your plan. Execute that plan and activate and apply in every aspect of your life. Review your philosophy, re-evaluate what sets you apart. Define your weaknesses and grow from it. Learn to work with others in your field. Connect with your customers daily. Find out what you could do better. Develop a relationship with those who support your business by being personal with your clients. Connect with yourself. Find and develop what you desire to discover about yourself. Starting a business is more than just about what services or products you provide but it's also about getting to know who you are and what you are capable of achieving in your life. Study to show yourself approved. When you don't study for success the likelihood of you making it is slim. Discover your compassion for charitable contribution. It's part of becoming successful. If you don't know how to give back, if you can't reach back and help someone else achieve and obtain then everything you have done is in vain. It's not just about you but all those around you. Your success can help others achieve their highest potential. People are attracted to those who achieve. If you are starting a business, seeking a promotion to your dream job or desire to be great in your marriage, or wonderful in parenting whatever your passion apply it to your life. When you get into the game of your life success will follow in every aspect. Take the time to thank those around you who have helped you obtain your success. People want to feel good no matter what. You want to be grateful for those who have helped you buy buying your products or services.   You want to help others feel empowered.   Your philosophy, your plan is about achieving so other can. Empowering others to invest in their marriage, their families, their business and taking the time to turn on their passion for living everyday. Develop your passion today. Take charge of your life and don't let anyone steal the vision that has placed in you. Remember it's your destiny. Live it….

Let's Review

1. Face the Truth about who you are
2. Know your weaknesses
3. Expect obstacles and hardship
4. Conquer your fears
5. Confront the demons in your closet that continue to keep you from succeeding.
6. Make a plan to overcome your past in every aspect of your life.
7. Write down your philosophy for your life, love, spiritual growth, parenting and contribution
8. Discover what will set you apart from your competition
9. Develop and Create a brand that will stand out above the rest
10. Change your inner script and the conversation within yourself.
11. Wake up daily with new goals to invest in your present and your future.
12. Change the way you feel and think about yourself.

13. Defeat insecurities by motivating yourself daily

14. Write down or use index cards to encourage yourself everyday.

15. Study and learn from those in your field.

16. Determine within yourself what you are willing to do to become successful.

17. Define what will make you great.

18. Put together a star team that will contribute to your dream.

19. Determine to help others achieve but reaching your goals.

20. Practice Your Role in which you desire to participate

21. Let go of your past, Let it go! It doesn't define your future

22. Get involved in your vision. Participate in your life.

23. Decided to transform your life by transforming your mind.

24. Perfect your image you are the first representation of your new business.

25. Always! Always! Have a business card.

26. Be ready when opportunity arise be ready to open the door.

27. When you have no other place to go dig a new path.

28. Challenge yourself to take steps everyday towards your goal.

29. Invest in yourself.

30. Invest in others. Teach, Train and Invest in others.

31. Love Yourself, Believe in Yourself and Embrace Your Dreams.

32. Write down goals daily.

33. Make a journal of your daily accomplishments and write down what you didn't accomplish and why.

34. Make a plan to accomplish your goals daily.

35. Be grateful in everyday living by participating in your life.

36. Get in the game.

37. Trust your instincts.

www.ingramcontent.com/pod-product-compliance
Lightning Source LLC
Chambersburg PA
CBHW030909180526
45163CB00004B/1761